Cultural Anthropology
FIELDWORK JOURNAL

Cultural Anthropology

FIELDWORK JOURNAL

Third Edition

KENNETH J. GUEST
BARUCH COLLEGE
THE CITY UNIVERSITY OF NEW YORK

W. W. NORTON & COMPANY
Independent Publishers Since 1923

W. W. Norton & Company has been independent since its founding in 1923, when William Warder Norton and Mary D. Herter Norton first published lectures delivered at the People's Institute, the adult education division of New York City's Cooper Union. The firm soon expanded its program beyond the Institute, publishing books by celebrated academics from America and abroad. By midcentury, the two major pillars of Norton's publishing program—trade books and college texts—were firmly established. In the 1950s, the Norton family transferred control of the company to its employees, and today—with a staff of four hundred and a comparable number of trade, college, and professional titles published each year—W. W. Norton & Company stands as the largest and oldest publishing house owned wholly by its employees.

Editor: Peter Lesser
Electronic Media Editor: Eileen Connell
Production Manager: Ashley Horna
Assistant Editor: Anna Olcott

Library of Congress Cataloging-in-Publication Data

Names: Guest, Kenneth J., author.
Title: Cultural anthropology : fieldwork journal / Kenneth J. Guest, Baruch
  College, the City University of New York.
Description: Third edition. | New York : W. W. Norton & Company, [2020] |
  Includes bibliographical references.
Identifiers: LCCN 2019042731 | **ISBN 9780393417227** (paperback)
Subjects: LCSH: Ethnology. | Applied anthropology.
Classification: LCC GN316 .G84 2020 | DDC 306—dc23
LC record available at https://lccn.loc.gov/2019042731

1 2 3 4 5 6 7 8 9 0

About the Author

Kenneth J. Guest is Professor of Anthropology at Baruch College, CUNY, and author of *God in Chinatown: Religion and Survival in New York's Evolving Immigrant Community.* His research focuses on immigration, religion, globalization, ethnicity, and entrepreneurialism.

Professor Guest's ethnographic research in China and the United States traces the immigration journey of recent Chinese immigrants from Fuzhou, southeast China, who, drawn by restaurant, garment shop, and construction jobs and facilitated by a vast human smuggling network, have revitalized New York's Chinatown. His writing explores the role of Fuzhounese religious communities in China and the United States, the religious revival sweeping coastal China, the Fuzhounese role in the rapidly expanding U.S. network of all-you-can-eat buffets and take-out restaurants, and the higher education experiences of the Fuzhounese second generation.

A native of Florida, Professor Guest studied Chinese at Beijing University and Middlebury College. He received his B.A. from Columbia University (East Asian Language and Cultures), an M.A. from Union Theological Seminary (Religious Studies), and an M.A., M.Phil., and Ph.D. from The City University of New York Graduate Center (Anthropology).

Contents

Preface

Cultural Anthropology: A Fieldwork Journal

Welcome to the exciting adventure we call fieldwork! This Fieldwork Journal is designed to give you a firsthand experience of how anthropologists go about their work. I hope these exercises, drawn from activities developed in my classroom, will reveal how fieldwork provides a valuable toolkit for gathering information to make decisions in your own life. Fieldwork skills and strategies can help you navigate the many unfamiliar or cross-cultural experiences you will encounter in this rapidly globalizing world, whether at work or at school, in your community, on the job, or in your family. And I hope you will see how key fieldwork strategies can help you become a more engaged and responsible citizen of the world.

Ethnographic fieldwork is the unique strategy that anthropologists—particularly cultural anthropologists—have developed to put people first as we analyze how human societies work. Chemists conduct experiments in laboratories. Economists analyze financial trends. Historians pore over records and library archives. Anthropologists start with people and their local communities.

Through fieldwork, we try to understand people's everyday lives, to see what they do and to understand why. We participate in their activities, take careful notes, conduct interviews, take photographs, and record music as we try to see the world through their eyes. We make maps of communities, both of the physical environment and of family and social relationships. Although careful observation of the details of daily life is the first step, through intensive fieldwork anthropologists look beyond the taken-for-granted, everyday experience of life to discover the complex systems of power and meaning that people construct to shape their existence, including gender, sexuality, race, ethnicity, religion, kinship, and economic and political systems. As we extend our analysis as anthropologists, we try to see how local lives compare to others and fit into larger human patterns and global contexts.

Fieldwork experience is considered an essential part of an anthropologist's training. It is the activity through which we learn the basic tools of our trade and hone those skills—careful listening and observation, engagement with strangers, cross-cultural interaction, and deep analysis of human interactions and systems of power and privilege. Through fieldwork we learn empathy for those around us, develop a global consciousness, and uncover our own ethnocentrism. Indeed, fieldwork is a rite of passage, an initiation into our discipline, and a common bond among anthropologists who have been through the experience.

So welcome to this Fieldwork Journal! I hope you will find fieldwork to be as eye-opening, thought-provoking, and life-changing as I have.

Ken Guest
New York
2020

Fieldwork: Tips for Getting Started

Fieldwork may seem unfamiliar or uncomfortable, especially meeting new people and crossing cultural boundaries. Here are some tips my students have found helpful for getting started.

1. **Prepare**
   Read about the people, organization, and place you will be visiting beforehand. Prepare interview questions. Gather tools for note-taking, photography, audio, and video recording. Be on time.

2. **Ask Permission**
   Seek informed consent from potential participants. Give them a chance to say yes or no. Be honest and direct about who you are and what you are doing.

3. **Participate and Observe**
   Participate in the group's activities to experience their lives from the inside. Beware your ethnocentrism—judging others based on your own cultural assumptions.

4. **Sit Still**
   Don't race in and out. Stay as long as you can, without wearing out your welcome. See what is actually happening rather than what you expected to find.

5. **Listen Carefully**
   Ask good questions and listen carefully to answers. Notice who is saying what to whom.

6. **Take Careful Notes**
   Write extensive notes, both during and after your fieldwork. Take note of seemingly unimportant matters, which may prove significant later.

7. **Notice Silences**
   What is not being said? Who is not in the room? Silences and absences reveal important insights but are difficult to notice.

8. **Map Inside and Out**

   Sketch the inside and outside of your fieldwork site, including both the place and the people. Sitting still and drawing may reveal unnoticed physical features and group dynamics.

9. **Embrace Being Insider and Outsider**

   While participating and observing inside a community, anthropologists simultaneously bring an outsider's perspective to analyze what they are seeing and experiencing.

10. **Leave Room for the Unexpected**

    Be patient, flexible, and open to the unexpected. Allow the ethnographic experience to develop on its own terms, not necessarily on your schedule.

11. **Be Open to Mutual Transformation**

    Your worldviews and those of people you study may be transformed by your fieldwork interactions.

12. **Return**

    Rapport and the quality of your research will deepen exponentially with each return visit.

13. **Protect Those You Study**

    Do no harm. Consider ways that things you learn could cause harm if you carelessly revealed them. Provide anonymity if necessary, masking names, places, and identifiers. Always ask permission.

14. **Say Thank You**

    Acknowledge people's generosity in sharing their time and stories with you. Find ways to return the generosity, perhaps by reporting back your findings.

15. **Analyze**

    Reflect on your fieldwork experience. What patterns emerge? What connections did you see between local and global? What dynamics of power and stratification did you find? What concepts in *Cultural Anthropology: A Toolkit for a Global Age* (or *Essentials*) help deepen your analysis?

Anthropology in a Global Age: Making a Can of Coke Unfamiliar

Anthropology's holistic, cross-cultural, and comparative approach can help us think more deeply about other people and cultures and live more consciously in our global world. As humans we take for granted many things about our lives and how the world works, whether it is our notions of race or the cheap cost of a bar of chocolate or a can of Coke. But anthropologists often describe how doing fieldwork can make the familiar strange and the strange familiar.

Conducting research across cultures helps develop our anthropological perspective. Beliefs and practices, which may at first seem strange, may become very familiar over time. The anthropological perspective can also enable us to perceive our own cultural activities in a new light. Even the most familiar aspects of our lives may then appear exotic, bizarre, or strange when viewed through the lens of anthropology. Through this cross-cultural training, anthropology offers the opportunity to unlock our ability to imagine, see, and analyze the incredible diversity of human cultures, including our own.

Our lives are entangled with things, what anthropologists refer to as *material culture*. Yet the stuff of our daily lives can become invisible—so familiar that we take it for granted. If we pay attention, however, stuff talks.

Take a can of Coke for instance. Coke is perhaps the most iconic item in American culture. And you can find Coke in almost every country in the world. But what do you really know about a can of Coke? What can you learn about yourself, your culture, and the world around you by considering this soft drink more carefully?

A can of Coke has a social life all its own. It is produced, distributed, and consumed. It moves about through space, is acted upon by others, and shapes people's lives in return. Igor Kopytoff suggested that all commodities—all things bought and sold—have a biography, and Arjun Appadurai urged anthropologists to consider the "social life of things." By this they mean that things, even very familiar things, tell a story that often reveals a great deal about who we are as humans, what we value, how our cultures work, and, in a time of increasing globalization, how the world works.

1

In the following exercise, try to look at a can of Coke through an anthropologist's eyes. Try to make something that is very familiar into something very strange by seeing beyond the label and the image to the complex set of human interactions that are organized around a can of Coke.

YOUR TURN

Buy a can of Coke and put it on your desk. Consider the following questions and gather data to help the story of a can of Coke come alive.

1. What is in it? Where did the ingredients come from?

_____

_____

_____

_____

_____

_____

_____

_____

2. Who made it? What is life like for those who made it?

_____

_____

_____

_____

_____

_____

_____

_____

_____

3. What is the impact of Coke on the local community where it is produced? Do they drink it? Do they work in the factory that makes it? How much do they earn? How much has the Coca-Cola factory changed their lives? Has it affected people in the community differently depending on their age, gender, or class?

_____

_____

_____

_____

_____

_____

_____

_____

_____

4. What is the impact of a can of Coke on the community where it is consumed? What are the health impacts? The environmental impacts? Where does the waste end up—landfills, the ocean, recycled, repurposed?

_____

_____

_____

_____

_____

_____

_____

_____

_____

_____

5. What do you pay for a 12-ounce can? What are the real social costs of producing a can of Coke—in terms of water, power systems, sewage treatment, pollution, garbage disposal, and roads for transportation? Who pays for these costs?

_____

_____

_____

_____

_____

_____

_____

6. What is the environmental impact of making a can of Coke, considering what it takes to grow and process ingredients such as high-fructose corn syrup, and how much water is required to produce the finished product?

_____

_____

_____

_____

_____

_____

By exploring the complex social life of a can of Coke, you are applying a set of analytical tools that may help you look more carefully and consciously at other familiar elements of culture.

Creating Culture: College Students and the Culture of Consumerism

Humans do not genetically inherit culture. We learn culture throughout our lives from the people and cultural institutions that surround us. Anthropologists call the process of learning culture *enculturation*. Some aspects of culture we learn from formal instruction: English classes in school, religious instruction, visits to the doctor, history lessons, dance classes. Other processes of enculturation are informal and even unconscious as we absorb culture from family, friends, and the media.

Culture is taught as well as learned. Humans establish cultural institutions—schools, medical systems, the government, media, and religious institutions—to enculturate their members. Their rules, regulations, laws, teachers, doctors, religious leaders, police officers, and sometimes militaries promote and enforce what is considered appropriate behavior and thinking.

This exercise is designed to help you think about how culture is created by considering the creation of a consumer culture. Twentieth- and early-twenty-first-century global capitalism is deeply tied to a culture of consumerism. In many parts of the world, consumerism has become more than an economic activity. It has become a way of life, a way of looking at the world—a culture. Key cultural rituals focus on consumption: holidays like Valentine's Day or Christmas, birthdays, weddings, and anniversaries promote the purchase of gifts. Advertising teaches us what we need to buy to fit in and be successful. And financial-services companies provide credit cards and loans to make sure we have access to the money to make our desires a reality.

College students are not immune to efforts to create a consumer culture. In fact, you are deeply immersed in it. Let's explore how.

Ask yourself what you need to have to feel like an average college student. Think about all the things you own. List your electronics (computer, smartphone, tablet, television, sound system) and your school supplies (books, notebooks, pens, calculator, backpack). Mentally go through your closets and dressers to list what you find there: clothes for different seasons and special occasions, accessories (bags, hats, belts, and shoes), and grooming items and cosmetics. List your mode of transportation, household furnishings, appliances, and so on. Once you have your list, assess what these things cost. Then ask yourself in each case whether these are things you *need* or things you *want*. For all the items that you identify as things you want more than absolutely need, ask yourself how the desire to acquire them—to consume them—was aroused and cultivated.

ITEM	COST	NEED/WANT	DESIRE TO CONSUME AROUSED BY: *

*Desire could be aroused by family, friends, parents, advertising, doctors, government, religious institutions, schools, something else, or a combination of factors.

continued on the next page

Continued from the previous page

ITEM	COST	NEED/WANT	DESIRE TO CONSUME AROUSED BY:

Now compare your list with the lists of your classmates, and continue your analysis with a few more questions.

1. Do you find differences in your lists based on gender, age, race, or ethnic identity?

_____

_____

_____

_____

_____

_____

_____

_____

2. Where were these things made? What does this suggest to you about globalization?

_____

_____

_____

_____

_____

_____

_____

_____

_____

Fieldwork: Mapping a Block

Often one of the first steps an anthropologist takes upon entering a new community is to map the surroundings. Mapping takes many forms and produces many different products. While walking the streets of a field site, the ethnographer develops a spatial awareness of where people live, work, worship, play, and eat, and of the space through which they move. After all, human culture exists in real physical space. And culture shapes the way space is constructed and used. Likewise, physical surroundings influence human culture, shaping the boundaries of behavior and imagination. Careful observation and description, recorded in maps and field notes, provide the material for deeper analysis of these community dynamics.

Develop your ethnographic skills of observation and description by drawing a map of a block or public space in your community and writing a narrative description of what you find.

Select an interesting location for your mapping project. You may choose to map a block defined as an area bounded on four sides by streets, as both sides of a single street (include the corners), or as the four corners of an intersection. Alternatively, you may choose to map an outdoor public space, such as a park or campus quadrangle, or an indoor space, such as a shopping mall or your college's student center. In these cases, focus on what is inside the space — that is, inside the building's four walls.

As a first step, spend time in your chosen location, paying attention to the details. Not all information presents itself immediately, so be patient. Spend an hour sitting and observing, taking careful field notes of your observations.

For an *outdoor space*, describe the streets, buildings, businesses, residences, schools, and hospitals. Make note of infrastructure like streetlights, sewers, telephone and electric lines, and satellite dishes as well as flows of people and transportation. For an *indoor space*, describe the rooms, offices, businesses, hallways, entry and exit locations, public and private areas, lighting, sounds, and smells. Also note the people—their activities, movements, and characteristics like gender, age, and race.

1. What location did you choose? What drew you to it? Describe what you found.

_____

_____

_____

_____

_____

_____

_____

_____

_____

2. What did you notice in your observations that you've never noticed before in your own regular, day-to-day interactions with the space?

_____

_____

_____

_____

_____

3. What is absent that you might have expected to find?

_____

_____

_____

_____

_____

4. Visit the same block or space at a different time of day or different day of the week. How do your observations vary over multiple visits?

_____

_____

_____

_____

_____

5. Now on the next page draw a map of the block or space, including the details you recorded. We are not all future architects or graphic artists, but take time to draw your map carefully. Use a pencil and ruler to begin. Add sketches and unique details. Consider adding colors and perhaps a legend to help your reader navigate the details of your map.

    If time permits, consider taking photos or shooting video of your location as part of your data gathering and to accompany your hand-drawn map. Consider asking people to tell you about the space you are mapping from their perspective. You might also expand your mapping project by examining census data at **http://projects.nytimes.com/census/2010/explorer**. Or consider searching local archives and databases to collect historical information or news articles about how your chosen location has changed over time.

    When presenting your mapping project, consider supplementing your hand-drawn map and narrative description with photos, Google Earth images, video clips, and statistical data. If you are working in a team, consider posting your research as a blog or wiki to promote collaboration, integrate multiple media sources, and enhance your presentation.

My map of: _____
(location name)

Language and Gender in the Classroom

Language comes alive when people communicate with one another. But languages are deeply embedded in the patterns of particular cultures. What people actually say and how they say it are intricately connected to the cultural context, to the speaker's social position, and to the larger systems of power within which the language operates. *Sociolinguistics* is the study of the ways in which culture shapes language and language shapes culture — particularly the intersection of language with cultural categories and systems of power such as age, race, ethnicity, sexuality, gender, and class.

This exercise will help you explore the intersection of language and gender in the classroom. The classroom is one of the most important places in which we learn social roles, including gender roles. We learn not only from the materials we read but also, and perhaps more important, from the people and the institutions around us. Talk is a key component of education. We learn through talking, thinking out loud, exploring new ideas with groups of people, and making ideas our own.

But studies have consistently shown that boys dominate classroom conversations. Boys speak more often, use more words than girls, and call out answers more frequently.[*] Classroom conditions also affect the action. Boys speak more when open classroom discussion allows them to just jump in. When teachers call on students by name, girls have a slight advantage. If the teacher calls on students in response to raised hands, boys again are favored, raising their hands more quickly and decisively.[†]

Joan Swann suggests that the unequal participation of boys and girls must be viewed in light of a wide variety of linguistic and nonlinguistic features that combine to create an environment in which boys feel more comfortable and secure to actively

---

[*] Myra Sadker and David Sadker, "Sexism in the Schoolroom of the '80s," *Psychology Today* (March 1985): 54–57.

[†] Joan Swann, "Talk Control: An Illustration from the Classroom of Problems in Analysing Male Dominance of Conversation," in *Language and Gender: A Reader*, ed. Jennifer Coates (London: Blackwell, 2007), 185–96.

participate in classroom talk. For instance, she notes that students in the classroom do not act alone; rather, they engage with a teacher who mediates and controls the dynamics; who calls on students directly; and whose body language, positioning, and gaze informally promote certain communication patterns. The classroom reflects larger cultural patterns according to which it may seem normal for males to talk more, leading to complicity by boys, girls, and the adults who teach them.

YOUR TURN

Can you see the dynamics of gender and language at work in your life? This week, choose one meeting of a class in which there is a fair amount of student participation and pay careful, analytical attention to the connections between gender and language in the classroom.

1. Keep a tally of how many times men speak and how many times women speak. Who speaks more often? Remember to take into account the proportion of men and women who are in the class.

MEN	WOMEN

2. How long, on average, do people speak? How many words do they use?

_____

_____

_____

_____

_____

3. What tendencies do you notice in the way men and women present themselves when speaking? Take note of body language and style of speaking.

MEN	WOMEN	BOTH

4. Now, turn your attention from the students to focus on the instructor. What is his or her role in encouraging or discouraging communication? Does the instructor's body language or gaze affect participation? How?

_____

_____

_____

_____

_____

_____

5. How often does the instructor call on men? Women?

_____

_____

_____

_____

_____

_____

6. Does the instructor's own gender seem to influence the way he or she interacts with members of the class? If so, how?

_____

_____

_____

_____

_____

_____

Initiating a Classroom Conversation about Race

Anthropologists find no scientific basis for classifications of race. Genetically, there is only one race—the human race, with all its apparent diversity. Yet despite consistent efforts over the last century by anthropologists and others to counter the inaccurate belief that races are biologically real, race has remained a powerful framework through which many people see human diversity and through which those in power organize the distribution of privileges and resources. Race—which is scientifically not real—has become culturally real in the pervasive racism found in many parts of the globe, including the United States.

Race is a deeply influential system of thinking that affects people and institutions. Over time, imagined categories of race have shaped our cultural institutions—schools, places of worship, media, political parties, economic practices—and have organized the allocation of wealth, power, and privilege at all levels of society. Race has served to create and justify patterns of power and inequality within cultures worldwide, and many people have learned to see those patterns as normal and reasonable. So anthropologists also examine racism: individuals' thoughts and actions as well as institutional patterns and policies that create or reproduce unequal access to power, privilege, resources, and opportunities based on imagined differences among groups.

Race and racism can be incredibly difficult topics of conversation in U.S. culture. How can the toolkit of anthropology help build relationships of rapport and trust that lead to deeper mutual understanding and opportunities for collective action? Addressing issues of race and racism requires first reflecting on race and racism in your own life and then opening up an honest conversation with others.

In your classroom or in another setting on campus—perhaps your dorm, a student organization, or a religious group—write down your personal reflections and recollections about race and racism as provoked by the following questions.*

1. What is your first recollection of race? Of encountering racism?

_____

_____

_____

_____

_____

_____

_____

_____

2. How would you describe the cultural environment in which you were raised: racially homogeneous? multiracial-multicultural? something else? How did the racial environment differ between your home/community and school?

_____

_____

_____

_____

_____

_____

_____

_____

_____

*Adapted from Carolyn Fluehr-Lobban, *Race and Racism: An Introduction*, 2nd ed. (Lanham, MD: AltaMira, 2018).

3. What patterns of race relations do you recall from high school? How much healthy social interaction was there across racial lines? What about interracial dating?

_____

_____

_____

_____

_____

_____

4. What patterns of race relations do you find on your college campus? Are they different from your experiences in high school? Have you encountered race and racism on campus?

_____

_____

_____

_____

_____

_____

5. Complete this sentence: The most important thing that our country needs to do *now* about race is _____

_____

_____

_____

_____

_____

6. What obstacles do you encounter in discussing and addressing race and racism?

_____

_____

_____

_____

_____

_____

After you reflect on these questions, form a discussion group with three or four other people. Try to make sure the group is racially inclusive. Read and discuss what you have written, giving everyone a chance to participate, before exploring your conversation further.

Seeing the Business of Ethnicity

Over a lifetime, humans develop complex identities that connect to many people in many ways. We build a sense of relationship, belonging, and shared identity through our connections to family, religion, hometown, language, citizenship, and more. Ethnicity is one of the most powerful identities that humans develop: It is a sense of connection to a group of people who we believe share a common history, culture, and (sometimes) ancestry and who we believe are distinct from others outside the group.[*]

Ethnicity can be seen as a more expansive version of kinship—the culturally specific creation of relatives—only including a much larger group and extending further in space and time. Anthropologists see ethnicity as a cultural construction, not as a natural formation based on biology or inherent human nature. And since we likely will never meet most people in our group, ethnic identification is primarily perceived, felt, and imagined rather than clearly documentable.[†]

Anthropologists examine the many ways ethnicities and ethnic identities can be invented, performed, and changed over time and according to one's social location. Ethnicity not only is mobilized to rally support in times of conflict but can also be mobilized to create opportunities, including economic opportunities. In today's global age, ethnicity is not only being experienced locally. It is also being creatively packaged and produced for a multi-billion-dollar global market: food, clothing, music, fashion, and cultural artifacts. People eat at ethnic restaurants, listen to ethnic music, and decorate their homes and offices with ethnic furnishings. Perhaps you have some "ethnic" items in your dorm or at home.

---

[*]Richard Jenkins, *Social Identity* (New York: Routledge, 1996); Ericksen, Thomas Hylland. *Ethnicity and Nationalism*, 3rd ed. (Boulder, CO: Pluto Press, 2010).
[†]Benedict Anderson, *Imagined Communities: Reflections on the Origin and Spread of Nationalism* (London: Verso, 1983).

But how exactly is ethnicity constructed and put to work? Let's consider that question by exploring an everyday setting near you: an ethnic restaurant.

Plan a fieldwork visit to a restaurant you identify with a particular ethnicity. It might be Chinese, Italian, Mexican, Indian, Greek, or any variation of ethnic restaurant easily accessible for your fieldwork. Before you visit, take a moment to think about what preconceived notions or expectations you already have about this group. Now visit the restaurant. Ordering some food is always an effective (and enjoyable) way to break the ice. Take a careful look around. How do you see ethnicity being expressed, performed, and put to work? Drawing on your skills of participant observation, take careful field notes.

1. **Overall Impression**. What makes you feel you are having an authentic "ethnic" experience?

   _____

   _____

   _____

   _____

2. **Food and Beverage**. Are there unique ingredients, styles of preparation, smells, colors, condiments, or desserts?

   _____

   _____

   _____

   _____

   Is the food presented in a special manner, with distinct platters, utensils, plates, or glasses?

   _____

   _____

   _____

   _____

3. **Staff**. What might be unique about their national origins, language use, clothing, mannerisms, greetings, or style of self-presentation?

_____

_____

_____

_____

_____

4. **Décor**. What do you notice inside or outside the restaurant about the architecture, signage, restaurant name, interior design, placemats, pictures, colors, lighting, music, or plants?

_____

_____

_____

_____

_____

5. **Other Observations**. What else do you notice?

_____

_____

_____

_____

_____

To dig deeper and begin to analyze your observations, request an interview with the owner or manager—someone who can provide an overview of the business. The following questions may help you explore strategic ways ethnicity is being put to work in the restaurant, used to attract customers, or mobilized to access co-ethnic business supply networks. The distinct expression of ethnicity in this restaurant might also reveal ways ethnicity may shift as people move from one place—perhaps country—to another.

6. What makes your restaurant unique in terms of ethnicity or cultural identity?

_____

_____

_____

_____

_____

7. How is this restaurant the same or different from ones in your place of origin?

_____

_____

_____

_____

_____

8. How do you think displays of ethnicity affect your restaurant's success?

_____

_____

_____

_____

_____

9. Where do you purchase your markers of ethnic identity: food, decorations, supplies, and equipment? Do you share an ethnic identity with your suppliers?

_____

_____

_____

_____

_____

10. How do you recruit staff? Do you draw on ethnic, social, or business networks?

_____

_____

_____

_____

_____

Ask if it would be appropriate to photograph elements of the restaurant that perform or represent ethnic identity.

Compare your field notes, pictures, and findings with a classmate. Compare the ways ethnicity has been constructed, performed, and put to work in your field sites.

After concluding your fieldwork, compare your pre-visit assumptions with what you actually observed. Do you see ways the restaurant owner might have anticipated your assumptions and expectations and put them to work to promote a sense of ethnic authenticity?

Cartoon Commercials and the Construction of Gender

Do you still watch cartoons on Saturday morning?

I want you to watch cartoons this weekend! Actually, I want you to watch the commercials that go along with the cartoons. These are directed at children who wake up early on Saturday mornings and plug in to the television or go online for a few hours until their parents get up. As you watch them, think about what lessons kids are learning about gender—about what it means to be female or male, feminine or masculine, in American culture.

From reading the gender chapter of *Cultural Anthropology: A Toolkit for a Global Age* (or *Essentials*), you know that we humans are born with biological sex but learn to be women and men. From the moment of birth, we begin to learn culture, including how to walk, talk, eat, dress, think, practice religion, raise children, respond to violence, and express our emotions like a man or a woman. We learn what kinds of behavior are perceived as masculine or feminine. Thus anthropologists refer to the cultural construction of gender. Family, friends, the media, doctors, educational institutions, religious communities, sports, and law all enculturate us with a sense of gender that becomes normative and seems natural. Over a lifetime, gender becomes a powerful, and mostly invisible, framework that shapes the way we see ourselves and others.

In this exercise, we consider the role of children's advertising in the development of gender identity. Children watch an average of 40,000 commercials a year on television.[*] This is a staggeringly high number, even though the Children's Television Act of 1990 limits commercials to 10.5 minutes per hour on the weekend and 12.5 minutes per hour on weekdays. (It jumps to 16 minutes per hour during prime time.) So kids watch a lot of commercials! But how do commercials shape the way kids think and feel?

---

[*]American Academy of Pediatrics, "Children, Adolescents, and Advertising," *Pediatrics* 118, no. 6 (2006): 2563–69.

Get up early one Saturday morning (I know this may be difficult!) and watch an hour's worth of cartoon commercials (or watch online). The following questions/prompts may help you analyze the construction of gender in cartoon commercials—to dig deeper into the gendering messages contained in both the form and content.

First decide who the target audience is in a particular commercial: boy or girl. You won't have a hard time with most (though some commercials are more generic). Then take notes on what you see.

	BOY COMMERCIALS	GIRL COMMERCIALS
What toys are advertised?		
What colors are emphasized?		
What do the kids do?		

What do the adults do?		
Where are the commercials set? Where does the action take place?		
What does the narrator/ voice-over sound like?		
Other insights?		

Judging by the messages of these commercials, what does it mean to be female or male, feminine or masculine, in American culture?

_____

_____

_____

_____

_____

_____

_____

_____

_____

_____

_____

_____

After making your lists, compare them with those of your classmates. Discuss how the media promote particular constructions of gender.

Attraction: Considering Chemistry, Meaning, and Power

Sexuality is a profound aspect of human life—one that stirs intense emotions, deep anxieties, and rigorous debate. The U.S. population holds widely varying views of where sexuality originates, what constitutes appropriate expressions of sexuality, and what its fundamental purpose is. It is fair to say that our cultural norms and mental maps of reality are in great flux and have been for several generations, in response to theological shifts, medical advances, and powerful social movements promoting the equality of women and gay, lesbian, bisexual, and transgender individuals. People sometimes think that sexuality is the most "natural" thing in the world. Ideas popular in American culture suggest that biological drives embedded in our genes during evolution shape our brain and instinctively control the body's hormones to ensure the reproduction of the species. Human sexuality and attraction are imagined to be rooted directly in bodily "chemistry."

But humans are a biocultural species. Our bodies and minds, which are not fully formed at birth, are shaped by the interaction of genes, environment, and culture. Beginning in the womb, our genes interact with the nutrients, sounds, emotions, and diseases that surround and infuse us to shape our bodies. The exact effects of the interaction of biology, culture, and environment are extremely difficult to measure, and this is particularly true in relationship to complex human sexual desires and behaviors.

For instance, we cannot predict a particular man's level of sexual desire for a particular partner by measuring his level of testosterone. Attraction, desire, and even lack of interest are not only biologically driven but also triggered by a vast array of cultural factors—including responses to the potential partner's age, religion, class, race, education, and employment prospects—or previous positive or negative experiences that may shape the body's physiological response to certain stimuli. So, although biology clearly plays a role in human sexuality, exactly how it manifests itself in each individual and how it interacts with the environment and culture is not as clear as many popular descriptions of sexuality suggest.

If, as anthropologist Eric Wolf argues, every relationship is embedded in complex dynamics of power, then sexuality is also more than an expression of individual desires and identities. French social scientist Michel Foucault described sexuality as "an especially dense transfer point for relations of power." By this he meant that in every culture, sexuality—like race, ethnicity, class, and gender—is also an arena in which appropriate behavior is defined, relations of power are worked out, and inequality and stratification are created, enforced, and contested.

What shapes your sexual desires, your attractions? How do you know who you would desire to have sex with? When I ask my students, inevitably somebody says, "Anybody!" But when we explore this further, it becomes clear that one's sexual desires, or sense of "chemistry," are not solely determined by chemicals—hormones, pheromones, testosterone, and dopamine. Sexual desires arise at the intersection of biology with the elaborate cultural system of meaning and power in which we live.

YOUR TURN

Consider the following attributes that my students often identify as key to making someone desirable or undesirable. What characteristics attract you or inhibit your attraction? Perhaps your first thoughts might go to "beautiful" or "handsome" or "sexy," but dig a little more to understand what those terms mean to you. How might a person's age, race, religion, class, education, health, politics, gender, or sexual identities affect your sense of their desirability?

Beauty	Race	Class	Legal status
Age	Ethnicity	Wealth	Health
Gender	Religion	Education	Hygiene
Sexual orientation	Kinship relationship	Language	Politics

1. Ask yourself which of these attributes are most important to you, and why?

_____

_____

_____

_____

_____

_____

_____

_____

_____

2. Researchers suggest our attractions are fluid—they may change over time or toward particular people. How have your attractions changed over time from childhood to youth to college student and how might they change over the rest of your life? Will the same attributes that attracted you as a 16-year-old attract you when you are 25 or 50? Which areas do you imagine to be most fluid and flexible over a lifetime? Least flexible? Is it solely biology or is attraction also shaped by the power of cultural norms and expectations, stereotypes, mental maps of reality, and implicit and explicit rules?

_____

_____

_____

_____

_____

_____

_____

3. After you have reflected on what shapes your own notion of attraction, discuss your findings with two or three classmates. What most surprised you?

_____

_____

_____

_____

_____

_____

_____

_____

_____

_____

_____

_____

Mapping Kinship Relationships: Tracing Your Family Tree

Kinship is constructed. Exactly how it is constructed varies from culture to culture. For example, families can be formed on the basis of biology, marriage, and/or choice. Thus strategies for building kinship and identifying relatives can be complicated. In this exercise, you will trace your family tree. Keeping in mind what you read in the kinship, family, and marriage chapter of *Cultural Anthropology: A Toolkit for a Global Age* (or *Essentials*), see what you can learn about how your family has constructed kinship relationships.

Research Strategies

In gathering information about your family history, many sources are available. Interview family members. Search family records to see what might already exist. Old family papers and record books can be very useful; for instance, family Bibles often have records written in them, and photographs may have names or dates noted on the back. Search for family burial plots; census and voter rolls; birth, marriage, and death certificates; wills; land deeds; and immigration and military records. Consult genealogy websites, and consider using an online program that allows members of your family to add information to your tree.

Getting Started

You will need a few tools to get started creating your own kinship chart. The following is a typical kinship chart of a nuclear family, labeled both with genealogical kin type and with the culturally specific kinship terms used in the United States. Your family may not fit this pattern, but it provides a place to start building your own family tree.

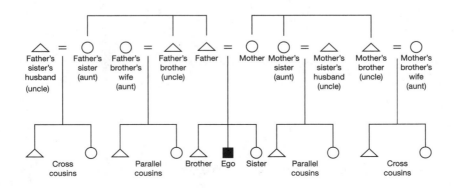

An abbreviated list of symbols used to create your genealogical kinship chart follows. The chart starts with a key individual, the central character, who is referred to as the "ego" and serves as the starting point in tracing kinship relationships. In your family tree, you are the ego.

Characters

SYMBOL	MEANING	SYMBOL	MEANING
△	male	/ (△, ⌀)	deceased
○	female	▲, ●, ■	ego of the diagram
□	individual regardless of sex		

Kin Abbreviations

SYMBOL	MEANING	SYMBOL	MEANING
M	mother	W	wife
F	father	D	daughter
B	brother	S	son
Z	sister	C	cousin
H	husband		

Relationships

SYMBOL	MEANING	SYMBOL	MEANING
=	is married to	|	is descended from
≠	is divorced from	⊓ (⊓)	is the sibling of
~	co-habitates with	⊙	adopted-in female
≁	is separated from / does not co-habitate with	⚠	adopted-in male

Kinship Language in Comparative Perspective

Language can tell you a lot about kinship. Anthropologists compare genealogical kin types to various cultures' actual kinship terms. For example, Americans use the term *uncle* to cover a wide range of kin, including a mother's brother (MB), a father's brother (FB), a mother's sister's husband (MZH), and a father's sister's husband (FZH). In this context, *uncle* does not differentiate biological descent from marriage relationships, nor does it distinguish by age.

In contrast, Chinese terminology calculates kinship much more carefully. It distinguishes paternal and maternal relatives, as well as birth order within generations and biological versus affinal descent. The Chinese do not have a generic term for *uncle*. Instead, unique terms denote a father's older brother as opposed to his younger brother. A distinction also exists between a father's brothers and a mother's brothers, as well as between a father's sister's husband and a mother's sister's husband.

> Father's older brother: *bofu* 伯父
> Father's younger brother: *shufu* 叔父
> Father's sister's husband: *gufu* 姑父
> Mother's brother: *jiufu* 舅父
> Mother's older sister's husband: *yifu* 姨父

Kinship terminology reflects different calculations within the culture about the role of these relatives in the life of the ego. In much of China, the extended family (*jia* 家) and lineage (*zu* 族) have played a pervasive role in economics, politics, and religion. As a result, kinship roles and obligations are carefully traced and implemented. (See a humorous but revealing explanation of the Chinese family tree at **http://bit.ly /GuestFieldworkJournal**.)

As you develop your own kinship chart/family tree, try using kin types rather than kin terms to make your family tree as specific and informative as possible. The simplicity of contemporary U.S. kinship terminology reflects the dominant role of the nuclear family that focuses on father, mother, and children as the key kinship relationships. Uncles and aunts, regardless of their genealogical kin type, play a limited role in child rearing, economic support, and inheritance. With kinship calculated bilaterally (that is, with equal weight on the mother's and father's sides of the kinship chart), there is no need to differentiate kinship terminology at this level.

1. Trace your family tree below, drawing on the research that you have conducted. Use the symbols in the table on page 35, and use the sample kinship chart as a model. Label each person, using both genealogical kin types and kinship terms. (You may want to use a pencil at the start so you can make updates and changes as you proceed.)

2. Families are more than lines on a family tree. As a budding anthropologist, you are interested in the patterns your family tree reveals. Families represent stories, interesting people, power dynamics—even mysteries. Your family tree may reflect educational patterns, geographic relocations, and inheritance flows. As you reflect on the process of mapping your kinship relationships, what stories does your family tree tell and what patterns does it reveal?

_____

_____

_____

_____

_____

_____

_____

_____

_____

_____

_____

_____

_____

_____

_____

_____

_____

_____

_____

_____

3. Even the process of preserving kinship history can be embedded in power dynamics. For instance, some branches likely are well preserved, and others might be missing. Who has been cultivating and pruning the tree, and who has the records now?

_____

_____

_____

_____

_____

_____

_____

_____

_____

_____

Ten Chairs of Inequality

Of all the systems of stratification and power, class may be the most difficult to see clearly and discuss openly in U.S. culture. A 2015 Gallup poll showed that 71 percent of Americans consider themselves to be middle or working class. Only 1 percent of respondents considered themselves to be upper class, and 13 percent upper-middle class. The remaining 15 percent considered themselves to be lower class.* Yet despite the U.S. national myth of a classless society, both quantitative and qualitative research studies expose the depth of inequality, stratified life chances, and obstacles to social mobility.

By *class*, anthropologists mean a system of power based on wealth, income, and status that creates an unequal distribution of the society's resources—usually moving wealth steadily upward into the hands of an elite. Systems of class stratify individuals' life chances and affect their possibilities for upward social mobility. *Social mobility* refers to one's change of class position—upward or downward—in stratified societies. *Life chances* refers to the opportunities that individuals have to improve their quality of life and realize their life goals. Life chances are determined by access not only to financial resources but also to social resources such as education, health care, food, clothing, and shelter. Class position—relative wealth, power, and prestige—determines access to these resources.

Income and wealth are key statistical indicators of class stratification in any society. Income includes what people earn from work, plus dividends and interest on investments, along with rents and royalties. In contrast, wealth is the total value of what someone owns—including stocks, bonds, and real estate—minus any debt, such as a mortgage or credit card debt. Income is unevenly distributed in the United States, and wealth even more so. If wealth were evenly distributed, every U.S. household would have had $692,100 in 2016. Do you know what your family's total wealth is?

---

*Gallup, "Fewer Americans Identify as Middle Class in Recent Years," April 8, 2015, www.gallup .com/poll/182918/fewer-americans-identify-middle-class-recent-years.aspx.

Although class stratification is not new, historical research suggests it is also not inevitable. By examining both statistical and ethnographic material, anthropologists seek to reopen a conversation about the roots of inequality—the obstacles to greater opportunity, social mobility, and improved life chances in a culture that is reluctant to discuss class.

YOUR TURN

To dramatize the distribution of wealth in the United States, find ten friends and ten chairs. Each chair will represent 10 percent of the nation's wealth, and each person will represent 10 percent of the population. Begin by placing one friend in each chair, making a straight row, to visualize what an even distribution of wealth would look like. Now ask the group to reallocate the chairs (reflecting wealth) to members of the group (representing total population) in response to each of the following prompts. Take a photo at each stage and ask the group members how they came to their arrangement.

1. What would you consider the ideal distribution of wealth in U.S. society?

_____

_____

_____

_____

_____

_____

_____

_____

_____

2. What do you think is the actual distribution of wealth in U.S. society?

_____

_____

_____

_____

_____

_____

_____

_____

_____

Now pick one of your friends and give her seven chairs. Ask your other nine friends to arrange themselves in the remaining three chairs. This arrangement shows the actual proportion of wealth held by the top 10 percent of the population. In fact, if your friend's arm represented the top 1 percent of the population, her arm alone would have more than three chairs (about 33 percent). To make this arrangement even more accurate, place one of your friends on the floor with no chair to represent the 10 percent of the population with negative wealth—more debt than assets. Ask how it feels to be in the group of nine, to be the one person in the top 10 percent, or to be sitting on the floor.

3. For the nine people sharing three chairs, what are the life chances of moving into the top 10 percent, where each would have seven chairs? What conditions would need to exist for that social mobility to happen?

_____

_____

_____

_____

_____

_____

4. Can you imagine being frustrated enough to revolt and take a few chairs by force? What keeps you from doing it?

_____

_____

_____

_____

_____

_____

Tracking the Travels of a Chocolate Bar

Do you know where your last chocolate bar came from?

Today's global economy is a complex network of exchanges and connections that reaches far beyond the candy machine outside your classroom or the store across the street. A piece of chocolate, a cup of coffee, or a smartphone links the wealthiest resident of a world capital or a student at an elite college to a subsistence farmer in Africa or a factory worker in China. In today's world, we are all deeply connected.

Anthropologists have often traced the movement of commodities such as silver, sugar, fur, tea, and coffee to reveal the global connections—political, economic, military, and social—that link producers and consumers, rural and urban communities, and people and nations on opposite sides of the world. For example, Sidney Mintz's classic work *Sweetness and Power: The Place of Sugar in Modern History** explores the way sugar historically transformed economic and social relations among Europe, Africa, and the Americas.

Tracing the movement of commodities illuminates the human dimensions of globalization that are often obscured by distance and marketing.

---

* Sidney W. Mintz, *Sweetness and Power: The Place of Sugar in Modern History* (New York: Viking Penguin, 1985).

Write a biography of a chocolate bar. Before you begin writing, gather some information about the chocolate bar's life. Buy one and put it on your desk. Now see if you can describe its life from the production of its ingredients until the moment you put it in your mouth. Consider the following questions:

1. What are the ingredients? (Perhaps start with cocoa, the primary ingredient.)

_____

_____

2. Where do the ingredients come from?

_____

_____

3. How are the ingredients produced?

_____

_____

4. What are the working conditions of the people who produce the cocoa?

_____

_____

5. How do the producers get the cocoa to market?

_____

_____

6. How are the prices set?

_____

_____

7. Which international corporations dominate the chocolate trade?

_____

_____

8. Who regulates the trade?

_____

_____

9. How is chocolate marketed?

_____

_____

10. Where did you buy your chocolate bar?

_____

_____

11. How much profit does a store owner make on a bar of chocolate?

_____

_____

12. Are there hidden costs that are not included in the price you paid? (Consider underpayment of labor; environmental impact; government subsidies that are direct [to the company] and indirect [infrastructure such as roads, ports, bridges, and water systems]; and the health care costs created by the harvesting, transporting, processing, and eating of this food.)

_____

_____

For further information, read the 2007 report *Hot Chocolate* produced by Global Witness, **www.globalwitness.org/sites/default/files/pdfs/cotedivoire.pdf**.

13. Now that you've gathered some information about the components of this chocolate bar, write its biography. Tell the story of its life from the farming of its ingredients to production and consumption.

_____

_____

_____

_____

_____

_____

_____

_____

_____

_____

_____

_____

_____

_____

_____

_____

_____

_____

A Day without Plastics

Plastics have revolutionized many aspects of human culture since their commercial development in the 1930s and 1940s. Today they are found in plastic bags, cosmetics, bottles, your phone, your clothes, your rugs, and even your jar of peanut butter. Most plastics are made from crude oil. They are lightweight, strong, and flexible, but they also never decay. Just over 90 percent of plastic waste has never been recycled. An international coastal cleanup day organized by the Ocean Conservancy prevented nearly 300 million pounds of plastics and other trash from escaping the shore into the ocean. By 2050, however, scientists estimate ocean plastics will outweigh ocean fish. A total of 9 billion tons of plastic has been generated since 1950, more than 1 ton for every person on the planet. By 2050, 13 billion tons will be in landfills or the environment.

With human consumption surpassing Earth's renewable resources and plastics overwhelming our oceans, rivers, beaches, and landfills and seeping into our food chain, efforts are emerging to reduce, reuse, and recycle plastics, particularly taking aim at single-use, disposable plastic items. Our culture and economy are built around high levels of consumption and easy disposal. But the environmental toll of this economic pattern on the planet and our individual lives has begun to outweigh its benefits.

In the United States, campaigns against plastic straw use have influenced many businesses to offer straws only on request or to switch to paper straws. The European Union plans to ban single-use cutlery, plates, straws, and drink stirrers by 2021. Britain has a 25-year plan to eliminate most plastic waste. Maybe you will be the one to invent an alternative to petroleum-based plastics, perhaps through a new technology like bio-plastics made from plant material.

Can you imagine a day without plastics?

Find out how much plastic you use in a day by conducting a personal audit. You may be surprised by how central plastic has become in your daily life. Start from the time you wake up to turn off your plastic alarm clock, wash your hair and brush your teeth in the bathroom, open your refrigerator, put on your clothes, change a diaper, ride transportation, go to school and work, buy your lunch, and go shopping. What about your electronics? How many plastic bottles, cups, straws, utensils, stirrers, resealable bags, shopping bags, and food containers or wrappers do you use? Take careful field notes.

_____

_____

_____

_____

_____

_____

_____

_____

Consider collecting all of the single-use, disposable plastic you use in a day, then take a picture to share with your classmates. Compare your findings and reflections with your classmates.

1. What surprises you the most?

_____

_____

_____

_____

_____

_____

2. What is the collective environmental impact of your class?

_____

_____

_____

_____

_____

3. How might you reduce, reuse, and recycle more plastics in your life? What would your plan be for living a day without plastics? Can you carry a "toolkit" with a non-plastic cup, cutlery, water bottle, and bag? What would it take to reduce your plastic waste by 50 or 75 percent? Can you change your behavior one day a year, a month, or a week?

_____

_____

_____

_____

_____

4. Plastic use is driven not only by individual consumption but also by corporate production. How might you, and your classmates, influence institutions, organizations, and corporations around you to increasingly reduce, reuse, and recycle plastics? Consider discussing with the manager or owner of your local restaurants, grocery stores, and coffee shops.

_____

_____

_____

_____

_____

5. At your college, consider asking the buildings and grounds department if you could work with them to conduct a plastics audit of the trash generated over the course of a day. Could your cafeteria or coffee shop reduce its plastic packaging? Can you help identify ways your college can reduce, reuse, and recycle plastics on campus?

_____

_____

_____

_____

_____

6. Investigate policy options for changing plastic use in your community, city, or state. What political efforts are under way to change policies and regulations about the production and consumption of plastics (perhaps focused on plastic bags, straws, cups, and food containers, or other non-recyclable plastics)? Are there student groups on your campus engaged in these issues?

_____

_____

_____

_____

_____

An Immigrant Interview

Humans have been on the move since our species' earliest days, seeking out better living conditions for themselves and their families. Humans eventually migrated out of Africa across continents into the Middle East, Europe, and Asia; they ultimately crossed oceans and land bridges to reach Australia and the Americas. Humans have moved in search of better hunting grounds, pastures, fields, natural resources, and climate. They have moved to avoid conflict, violence, predators, and natural disasters. Some, such as early explorers Marco Polo and Ibn Battuta, traveled long-distance trade routes that linked much of the world well before Columbus's time. Others were forced to move against their will—for example, to serve the needs of colonialism on plantations and in mines, including millions in the trans-Atlantic slave trade. Clearly, movement is a fundamental characteristic of the human experience.

The past 30 years have seen one of the highest rates of global migration in modern history, not only between countries but within them as well. The powerful effects of globalization have stimulated migration from rural areas to urban areas and from less-developed countries to more-developed countries. At the same time, time-space compression has transformed the migration experience: Rapid transportation and instantaneous communication enable some migrants to travel more cheaply and quickly, while remaining connected with folks back home, in ways that were impossible for earlier migrant generations.

But why do people migrate? And why do they choose certain destinations? These decisions are rarely random or frivolous. In fact, most people in the world never migrate.

The decision to migrate requires the confluence of a variety of factors—factors that anthropologists identify as *pushes* and *pulls*, *bridges* and *barriers*. People are pushed to migrate from their home community by poverty, famine, natural disasters, war, ethnic conflict, genocide, disease, and political or religious oppression. But destinations are not chosen randomly, nor are all destinations equal. Immigrants are pulled to certain places by job opportunities, higher wages, educational opportunities for themselves and their children, access to health care, or investment opportunities. To further understand global migration, we must look beyond the push and pull factors to examine the bridges and barriers that influence who moves and where the movers go—the factors that enable or inhibit migration.

YOUR TURN

To deepen your understanding of the immigrant experience, interview an immigrant of any age, gender, and nationality. Ask to hear his or her immigration story. Listen for the key migration concepts discussed in this chapter: pushes and pulls, bridges and barriers, and immigrant types. Ask about the person's incorporation experience in the new country: How did they learn the language or find a job, housing, health care, legal advice, education, and a religious community? How are gender roles different in the new country? What are the expectations of members of the second generation, and how do their lives differ from those of their immigrant parents? Be sure to take detailed notes in the space below and on the following page. Analyze this story, and then on the pages that follow synthesize it in a short essay using the first person.

Interview Notes:

Interview Notes (continued):

Essay:

_____

_____

_____

_____

_____

_____

_____

_____

_____

_____

_____

_____

_____

_____

_____

_____

_____

_____

_____

_____

Essay (continued):

_____

_____

_____

_____

_____

_____

_____

_____

_____

_____

_____

_____

_____

_____

_____

_____

_____

_____

_____

_____

_____

_____

_____

_____

Essay (continued):

_____

_____

_____

_____

_____

_____

_____

_____

_____

_____

_____

_____

_____

_____

_____

_____

_____

_____

_____

_____

_____

_____

Making the State Real

Power is often described as the ability or potential to bring about change through action or influence—either one's own or that of a group or institution. This may include the ability to influence through force or the threat of force. Power is embedded in many kinds of social relations, from interpersonal relations, to institutions, to structural frameworks of whole societies. Power is deeply embedded in culture, including systems of power such as race and racism, ethnicity and nationalism, gender, human sexuality, economics, and family.

Eric Wolf urged fellow anthropologists to see power as an aspect of all human relationships. All human relationships have a power dynamic. Though cultures are often assumed to be composed of groups of similar people who uniformly share norms and values, in reality people in a given culture are usually diverse and their relationships are complicated. Power in a culture reflects stratification—uneven distribution of resources and privileges—among participants. Some people are drawn into the center of the culture. Others are ignored, marginalized, or even annihilated. Power may be stratified along lines of gender, racial or ethnic group, class, age, family, religion, sexuality, or legal status.

When considering political power in relationship to the state, anthropologists examine how the state becomes the ultimate authority within a particular territory. While overt means of coercion, like police and the military, may appear to be the most obvious answers, the exertion of authority by the state is a much more complicated matter. Anthropologists suggest that the state becomes real in the imaginations and experiences of people as it is encountered in a particular space. This spatialization of the state*—the perception that the state fills a particular space, encompasses all aspects of culture, and stands above all other elements of society—is produced through mundane bureaucratic state practices. The state is encountered in everyday

---

*James Ferguson and Akhil Gupta, "Spatializing States: Toward an Ethnography of Neoliberal Governmentality," *American Ethnologist* 29, no. 4 (2002): 981–1002.

acts of governance: mail delivery, tax collection, mapping, surveys, passport issuance, jury duty, voting notarization, distribution of food to the poor, distribution of pension checks to the elderly. Through these routine and repetitive acts, the state comes to feel all-encompassing and overarching.

YOUR TURN

Anthropologists James Ferguson and Akhil Gupta (2002) suggest the state, which may seem very abstract, becomes real in the imaginations and experiences of people as it is encountered in daily life. How does the state become real for you? Keep a diary of the ways you encounter the power of the state—federal, state, and local—in any given day. Use the following categories to get started. Can you identify at least 25 daily encounters with the state?

Food: How does the state regulate and shape the food you eat? Are there labels on your food that indicate the presence of the state? What do they say? If you eat out, how does the state regulate the restaurant, its food preparation, and its employees? What role does the state play in regulating trash disposal or recycling?

_____

_____

_____

_____

_____

_____

People: Note the public employees you encounter in a day. Are they wearing uniforms? How does their job shape and influence your life? Were there more public employees in your life than you expected or fewer?

_____

_____

_____

_____

Transportation: When you are traveling around your city or town, observe the ways the state shapes your experience. What kinds of signs, rules, and fees do you encounter? What investment has the state made in transportation infrastructure like roads, stoplights, buses, or trains?

_____

_____

_____

_____

_____

_____

School: How does the state shape your school experience? What role does the state play in determining what you are taught? What role does the state have in how you pay for your education? What funding does the local, state, or federal government provide your school?

_____

_____

_____

_____

_____

_____

Infrastructure: How does the state support your daily needs like water, electricity, trash removal, clean streets, and public safety?

_____

_____

_____

_____

_____

Public Agencies: Describe local, state, and federal agencies and offices that shape your day.

_____

_____

_____

_____

_____

Social Life: How does the state shape your social life? Consider age restrictions or other regulation of activities like driving, drinking, marijuana use, sex, and marriage.

_____

_____

_____

_____

_____

Media: What is the state's role in media like television, radio, the internet, news, or social media?

_____

_____

_____

_____

_____

_____

_____

Safety: What role does the state play in ensuring your safety, and how do you encounter that over the course of the day? How is your life shaped by police, firefighters, fire codes, gun laws, environmental protections, school security, or other people or regulations?

_____

_____

_____

_____

_____

_____

Absence: In what aspects of your life do you feel the state is absent? Is this beneficial or detrimental? How would a stronger state presence change this part of your life?

_____

_____

_____

_____

_____

_____

Visit to a Religious Community

Religion plays a central role in human life and human culture. Through the study of religion, anthropologists engage some of the deepest, most difficult, and most enduring human questions—about meaning, difference, power, love, sexuality, mortality, morality, human origins, and kinship. Religion has been a central interest of anthropologists since the beginning of our field. Research about religious beliefs and practices worldwide has explored an amazing diversity of symbols, rituals, myths, institutions, religious experts, groups, deities, and supernatural forces.

Religion is a set of beliefs and rituals based on a unique vision of how the world ought to be, often focused on a supernatural power, and lived out in community. As social scientists, anthropologists have largely been uninterested in questions of any religion's ultimate truth or falsity. Instead we understand that religious worlds are real, meaningful, and powerful to those who live in them. Our task is to carefully make those worlds come alive for others by capturing their vivid inner life, sense of moral order, dynamic public expressions, and interactions with other systems of meaning and power.

Religion offers a rich vein of material for exploring the complexity of human culture, including systems of belief and systems of power. It is perhaps the hottest topic in the world today as globalization brings different traditions, beliefs, and practices into contact. In the United States, immigration over the past five decades has transformed the religious landscape. Temples, mosques, gurdwaras, and retreat centers now join churches and synagogues in small towns and big cities across the country. College campuses, too, reflect an expanding religious diversity. As people of different religious traditions encounter one another in neighborhoods, schools, and other public institutions, lively debates take place about education, zoning, health care, public security, and civil rights. These encounters create the potential for tension and misunderstanding on school boards, zoning committees, and town and city councils, as well as in civic associations and even college classrooms. But they also offer opportunities for interfaith encounters, learning, and engagement.

An anthropological understanding of religion can help you navigate and engage this changing landscape.

To deepen your understanding of religion, choose a religious community that you would like to visit, either by yourself or with other members of your class. Contact the organization to arrange a visit at a time when you can participate in a public ritual, perhaps a worship service, festival, or parade. Be sure to find out what attire is appropriate for visitors.

During your visit, consider how the concepts introduced in this chapter can serve as tools for analyzing and understanding what you see.

1. Do you see examples of sacred and profane objects or acts? List them below. (You may need to investigate Émile Durkheim's work on the sacred and profane as described in the religion chapter of *Cultural Anthropology: A Toolkit for a Global Age* [or *Essentials*].)

SACRED	PROFANE

2. Can you recognize ways in which ritual promotes a sense of communitas by leading members through separation, liminality, and reincorporation? (You may need to investigate Victor Turner's work on ritual as described in the textbook.) In the following boxes, describe the stages of ritual that you see.

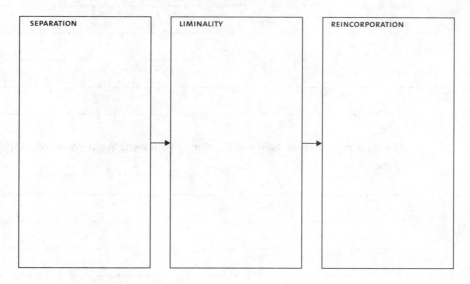

| SEPARATION | LIMINALITY | REINCORPORATION |

3. Can you identify particular symbols unique to this religious community and determine their meaning? What do you think gives them their power and authority? (You may need to investigate Clifford Geertz and Talal Asad's work on symbols in religion, as described in the textbook.)

_____

_____

_____

_____

_____

_____

4. In the textbook, review Karl Marx's critique of religion as "the opium of the people." Is Marx's perspective relevant to the event you're attending? In what way?

_____

_____

_____

_____

_____

5. How does power make itself evident during your visit? What power relationships do you observe?

_____

_____

_____

_____

_____

6. Can you identify any ways in which globalization influences the religious beliefs and practices that you observe?

_____

_____

_____

_____

_____

If appropriate, interview a religious leader or a member of the religious community during your visit. Use the interview to explore these questions further and to gain deeper insight into what you observe.

What Do You Do When You Get Sick?

Medical anthropologists have dedicated significant effort to documenting healing practices and health systems around the globe, from indigenous and tribal communities and urban metropolises to farming communities and groups of migrant workers. In the process they have identified a vast array of ideas about the causes of health and disease, different notions of the body, and varied cultural strategies to address pain, cure illness, and promote health. One key finding is that these beliefs and practices are intricately intertwined with the way local cultures imagine the world works and the relationship of an individual's body to his or her surroundings.

In assessing how disease and health conditions affect specific populations and how specific cultural groups diagnose, manage, and treat health-related problems, medical anthropologists have found it useful to distinguish between disease, illness, and sickness. A disease is a discrete, natural entity that can be clinically identified and treated by a health professional. A disease may be caused genetically or through infection by bacteria, a virus, or parasites. But the bacteria, viruses, or parasites are the same regardless of location or cultural context. Illness, however, is more than the biological disease. Illness is the individual patient's experience of being unwell—the culturally defined understanding of disease. It includes the way the person feels about it, talks about it, thinks about it, and experiences it within a particular cultural context. Disease can be observed, measured, and treated by sufferers and healers. But culture gives meaning to disease, shaping the human experience of illness, pain, suffering, dying, and death.*

---

*Merrill Singer and Hans A. Baer, *Introducing Medical Anthropology: A Discipline in Action* (Lanham, MD: AltaMira, 2007).

Sickness refers to the individual's public expression of illness and disease, including social expectations about how one should behave and how others will respond. Being sick may release the sick person from social obligations like work, school, or parenting. But sickness also requires the patient to perform a certain "sick role" in order to receive the corresponding social support.

People recognize widely different symptoms, illnesses, and causes for health challenges and have developed widely different strategies for achieving and maintaining health. Though the stereotypical Western images of health care often revolve around doctors in white coats, dentists' chairs, hospitals, strong medications, and advanced technology (such as X-rays, MRIs, and CT scans), medical anthropologists have found that these are not the primary points of access to health care for most people in the world. Rather, before seeking the assistance of a trained medical professional, people everywhere apply their personal medical knowledge, their own strategies—often handed down within families or communities—for dealing with disease, illness, pain, and discomfort.

Interview a classmate about his or her strategies for getting healthy or staying healthy. The following questions may help you assess your colleague's understanding of health, disease, illness, and proper health care.

1. Whom do you consult? Do you call your mom, dad, doctor, pharmacy, health food store, pastor, friends, massage therapist, chiropractor, campus health center, hospital? Someone else?

_____

_____

_____

_____

_____

2. What strategies do you use to get well? Do you sleep, drink orange juice, eat chicken soup, take vitamin C, get antibiotics? Do you starve a cold and feed a fever? Do you follow practices from a culture outside the United States?

_____

_____

_____

_____

_____

3. What strategies do you use to relieve pain? Do you take medications for fever, headache, cough, and runny nose or do you let them run their course? Do you take over-the-counter pain relievers or get a doctor's prescription for something more powerful? Do you apply heat or ice? Do you ask for a massage?

_____

_____

_____

_____

_____

4. Are your healing strategies specific to your family, ethnic group, religious affiliation, or local or national context?

_____

_____

_____

_____

_____

5. Are your healing strategies guided by moral, economic, religious, or legal mandates or constraints—for instance, about the use of alcohol, medical marijuana, or narcotics?

_____

_____

_____

_____

_____

6. How do you figure out what made you sick so that you don't get sick again? Do you wash your hands more often? Use hand sanitizer? Filter or boil your water? Consult an older adult, a doctor, or an online source such as WebMD?

_____

_____

_____

_____

_____

7. When you are sick, how do you keep others from being infected? Do you cover your mouth when you sneeze? Do you stop hugging and kissing your friends and loved ones? Do you take medications or other preparations more regularly?

_____

_____

_____

_____

_____

8. How do you feel about getting sick? What do you think getting sick says about you as a person? What does it say about you if you have certain symptoms: cold, fever, diarrhea, a sexually transmitted infection?

_____

_____

_____

_____

_____

_____

9. Is there a social cause of your illness or disease? Does it result from poor hygiene by others, lack of clean water, or improper food inspection or preparation? Does a stigma about the illness or disease keep you from seeking treatment? Is treatment too expensive for you? Is it too difficult for you to access health care (for example, too far away)?

_____

_____

_____

_____

_____

Now consider your own experience of health, disease, illness, and sickness.

10. How would you respond to the questions you asked your classmate?

_____

_____

_____

_____

11. How did you learn your health strategies?

_____

_____

_____

_____

12. Is there a certain way you are expected to behave—a sick role—in order to take a sick day or miss a class? Do you need to stay home for a certain period of time, see a doctor, or produce a note?

_____

_____

_____

_____

13. Can you imagine that someone from another culture might have strategies and responses that are very different from but just as effective as yours?

_____

_____

_____

_____

Conducting an Ethnography of Art

Anthropologists define art broadly as all the ideas, forms, techniques, and strategies that humans employ to express themselves creatively and to communicate their creativity and inspiration to others. Art may include a vast array of paintings, drawings, weavings, photographs, film, sculpture, architecture, dance, music, songs, games, sports, clothing, and cuisine. But art is not limited to the artists. Art is both created and received. Cooking and building, fashion and oratory, decorating and dressing, sewing and play all represent media through which artists and audience communicate. Through these often dynamic encounters, art takes its shape not only in creation but also in perception.

Anthropologists' unique approach to art includes particular attention to how art is embedded in community—how art connects to social norms and values and economic and political systems and events. Who makes it and why? What does it mean to the people who create it and to those who perceive it? What are its functional and inspirational roles? As ethnographers, anthropologists of art attend not only to the form of the art itself—its designs, movements, and sounds—but also to its context. They consider not only the creative production of a piece of art but also each work's unique and often complex history as it journeys through human culture. After all, art is embedded in everyday exchanges, social networks, business negotiations, and other struggles over profit, power, and prestige.

Placing art in context has become more complicated and interesting in recent years. Today, in an era of intensifying globalization, local art is created in a global landscape. Local art practices, objects, and events intersect with global movements of people and ideas. Art is often a key juncture through which local communities engage the global economy. Within this global "artscape,"* the creation of local art may provide not only a means of economic activity but also a venue to demonstrate

---

*Arjun Appadurai, ed., *The Social Life of Things: Commodities in Cultural Perspective* (Cambridge: Cambridge University Press, 1986).

cultural skills and values and to assert local cultural identity in the face of rapid change. As a result, contemporary anthropologists of art explore the journeys of objects across boundaries and the implications of the "traffic in culture" for both those who produce art and those who consume it.[†]

YOUR TURN

To develop your skills as an ethnographer of art, select a piece of art. It can be any object, event, or other expressive form. You might choose a reproduction of urban life, wood carving, mud sculpture, acrylic painting, fashion, dance, music, procession, kids' game, documentary film, or museum display. You might also choose a banquet, a parade, a festival, a concert, or a religious ritual.

My piece of art is

_____

Now get out your anthropological toolkit. Approach your piece of art as an ethnographer. Participate in it. Observe it. Assess its content. Interview the artist or the audience. Consider the following questions to stimulate your thinking.

[†] George E. Marcus and Fred R. Myers, *The Traffic in Culture: Refiguring Art and Anthropology* (Berkeley: University of California Press, 1995).

1. As a form of communication, art is meant to evoke emotional responses (laughter, crying, melancholy, or joy) as well as intellectual responses to its shape, order, and form. The artistic message may be intended to teach or inspire, to engage in an exchange about values, goals, standards, and imagination of the artist and community. It may commemorate individuals, groups, events, or deities and attempt to create enduring messages or memories. Or it may seek to provoke action, influence events, or inspire social change. How does your piece of art communicate, evoke, or inspire? What do you think the artist was trying to say with his or her work?

_____

_____

_____

_____

_____

2. As you consider your object, event, or experience, take some time to carefully describe the elements of the art.

_____

_____

_____

_____

_____

3. How do people interact with the art and why?

_____

_____

_____

_____

_____

4. Consider your art object's history, its role in the local community, and its connections beyond the local community. Where did this piece of art come from? Has it moved across geographic space? Who paid for it, bought it, developed it? Can it be sold?

_____

_____

_____

_____

5. See how the piece of art is embedded in relationships of power. Who told you it was "art"? Who controls it? If it is displayed, who designed the display and determined how it would be contextualized?

_____

_____

_____

_____

6. How might the artwork you have chosen allow certain people to form or maintain relationships of power or assert particular ideas about how relationships of power are organized?

_____

_____

_____

_____

7. Compare notes with some classmates. With all the information you have gathered, see if you can collectively develop a universal definition of art. Try to limit yourself to one sentence!

_____

_____

_____